OBJECT LESSONS FOR A YEAR

52 Talks for the Children's Sermon Time

DAVID J. CLAASSEN

BAKER BOOK HOUSE
Grand Rapids, Michigan 49506

Published by Baker Books
a division of Baker Publishing Group
P.O. Box 6287, Grand Rapids, MI 49516-6287
www.bakerbooks.com

ISBN: 978-8010-2514-3

Printed in the United States of America

12   13   14   15   16   30   29   28   27   26   25

To
Diann.
She is
a living and positive object lesson
for our two children,
Julie and Danny

Contents

Introduction

Object lessons are certainly not a new idea. Jesus frequently used common, everyday objects to drive home a point: rocks, birds, seeds, flowers, water, bread, coins, and many other things.

The objects used in this series of lessons are rather easy to come by. I imagine that many pastors, if they are like me, wait until Saturday before finally entering into a desperate search for a children's object lesson for Sunday morning. I hope some of these lessons can bail you out under such conditions. However, it might be wise to quickly skim the list of objects needed ahead of time as some of them are seasonal, especially those found in nature. For some of the objects you may have to consult members of your congregation.

I have written the object lessons in the style in which I have used them on television and with the children of my own congregation. Your style may be different. My presentation is only a suggestion of one way it can be done.

May you, the children of your church, and your adult church members find these object lessons enjoyable and helpful!

1

Rooted in Jesus

Objects Needed

One cut flower and one potted flower.

Theme

If we want to stand up under the troubles in life we must be rooted in Christ.

Presentation

I have two flowers with me today. One of the flowers is a cut flower. It is meant to be placed in a vase with water. The other flower is a potted plant.

One of these flowers will last much longer than the other. It will also be able to hold up better under bad conditions. Do you know which one I'm talking about? (Allow them to answer.) That's right, it's the potted plant that will last longer. It is better off because it has roots! The cut flower will only last a few days and then will have to be thrown out because it has been cut off from its roots.

The Bible says that if we want to be the good and wonderful people God intends us to be, we must be rooted—rooted in Jesus Christ. Now of course the Bible doesn't mean we should have actual roots. It means that we should be very close to Jesus, sticking by him at all times. Being rooted in Jesus means we depend on him.

Jesus will give us the strength to handle problems. We won't have to wilt in tough situations like this cut flower will do eventually. We can be like the potted flower and keep on living the good life God wants us to because we are rooted in Jesus.

I'm sure you each have some problems right now. Your problems may have to do with grades at school, friends, or maybe parents. All of us have problems, including me. But if we stay close to Jesus—stay rooted in him—we'll turn out OK.

Key Text

"So then, just as you received Christ Jesus as Lord, continue to live in him, rooted and built up in him, strengthened in the faith as you were taught, and overflowing with thankfulness." (Col. 2:6-7)

2

Thermostat or Thermometer?

Objects Needed

Thermometer and a thermostat (you can pick up a discarded one from a furnace repairman).

Theme

We can make events in life happen *for* us instead of letting them happen *to* us!

Presentation

Do you know what this is? (Holding up the thermometer, let someone answer.) That's right, it's a thermometer. When you read a thermometer, it tells you what the temperature is.

This other object also detects temperature but it has a slightly different job. It's a thermostat. You probably have one on a wall at home. It tells your furnace when to go on and off. It not only reads the temperature in a room but it does something about it!

What I want to say today is: be a thermostat in life, not just a thermometer!

A thermometer-type person simply goes along with what's happening. If everybody in the group of people he is with is happy, he is happy. If they are angry, he is angry. If they are doing something wrong, the thermometer-type person will go along with it and do the same thing even though it's wrong. If a situation is discouraging, everybody is discouraged.

A thermostat-type person is completely different. If you are this kind of person it means you decide how you *ought* to think or act, not how you *want* to think or act! Being a thermostat means you try to change the situation for the better. If you are with your friends you will try to influence them to do good instead of letting them influence you to do bad.

A thermometer lets the temperature in the room change it. A thermostat changes the temperature of the room!

Be a thermostat. Don't just let life happen to you in any old way. Make life happen for the good, for yourself and for those around you.

Key Text

"Do not conform any longer to the pattern of this world, but be transformed by the renewing of your mind." (Rom. 12:2)

3

Be a Filter!

Objects Needed

A coffee filter.

Theme

Of all the things we see, hear, and think we must only accept within us those that are good, filtering out the rest.

Presentation

This coffee filter can teach us a very important lesson on how to live a better life.

Can anyone tell me how a coffee filter works? First you place the filter in a special bowl that comes with your coffee pot. You then place some ground coffee into the filter. The coffee maker works by pouring a stream of hot water over the ground coffee. The filter lets the coffee-flavored water through, but not the coffee grounds. If there is one thing your parents don't like to see in their coffee it's coffee grounds. It's the job of the filter to keep them out.

There are many other kinds of filters. Furnace filters keep the dust out of the air we breathe. Gas filters keep the gas in our cars clean. Although filters come in all shapes and sizes and filter all kinds of things, they

14

have one thing in common: they filter out something that shouldn't be let through.

Did you know that you and I should be filters? That's right. God wants us to filter all the different things we hear, see, and think. For instance, at school you will hear some kids say bad words. Should you keep those words in mind and say them sometime? Of course not. You should filter those out and not let them settle down in your mind. When you see someone do something that is wrong, should you go ahead and do it just because they did? No, I'm sure you realize you shouldn't. You must filter that out and say, "That is not something I want to do because I know it's wrong." When you think a bad thought you can use your filter inside of you again. Just tell yourself, "I'm not going to keep thinking that bad thought. I'm going to think about something else."

Just as the coffee filter won't let coffee grounds into the coffee pot, so you and I should filter out what comes our way and only accept inside of us those things that are good and pleasing to God. Be a good filter, OK?

Key Text

"Finally, brothers, whatever is true, whatever is noble, whatever is right, whatever is pure, whatever is lovely, whatever is admirable—if anything is excellent or praiseworthy—think about such things." (Phil. 4:8)

4

The Power of Words

Objects Needed

Tube of toothpaste, plate.

Theme

A word is much like toothpaste. Once you let it out you can't take it back.

Presentation

I need a volunteer to do two things. First, take this tube of toothpaste and squeeze quite a large quantity out onto this plate. That's good. Now I want you to put the toothpaste back into the tube!

What seems to be the problem? Can't you stuff it back in? Well, I know I've asked you to do the impossible. Once toothpaste is out of the tube you can't put it back.

Words are much like this toothpaste. Once we let them out of our mouths we really can't take them back.

This means we should be careful of the words we let out of our mouths. For instance, some of the things we say about a person may not be true. Some of the words we say when we are angry aren't very nice and we don't really mean what we say. It's at times like this that we ask the person we have hurt to forgive us. But even if the person forgives us he or she will have a hard time forgetting what we said. There is nothing you or I can do to completely take back something terrible we have said. It's like too much toothpaste being squeezed from the tube!

Being able to say words and communicate thoughts and ideas is a marvelous gift from God. Let's not misuse this wonderful ability by speaking words that hurt people.

Ask Jesus to help you control your tongue. Ask him to help you say only the things you should say.

Remember, a word is a lot like toothpaste—once you let it out you can't take it back.

Key Text

"And whatever you do, whether in word or deed, do it all in the name of the Lord Jesus." (Col. 3:17)

5

Let God Change You

Objects Needed

An electric fan (plugged in) and a pinwheel.

Theme

We're able to see God working when we let him influence and move us.

Presentation

I would like a boy to put his hand in front of this fan. (Have fan turned on.) Do you feel anything? (Let child respond.) You mean you feel a breeze? I don't see any breeze or wind. Are you certain you feel it?

Wind is invisible. You know you feel it but how can you prove it's really there to someone who doesn't believe you? Could this pinwheel help? (Let child put the pinwheel in front of the fan.) Yes! Now I can see that there is a wind because I see it turning the pinwheel. (Turn off fan.)

The only way you can "see" the wind outside is by what it moves—trees, windsocks, or flags, for instance. When they are moving you know there's a wind.

Did you know that the original name for the Holy Spirit was *wind*? That's right. The old Hebrew word for spirit means wind.

18

We read in the New Testament that when Jesus left earth and the Holy Spirit came there was a mighty wind. We also know that when you believe in Jesus and accept him as your Savior, his Holy Spirit lives inside of you. I hope you feel God's Holy Spirit close to you, loving you and helping you.

One of the hardest things to do is let others see God in us. How can you and I prove that Jesus is inside of us, that his Holy Spirit is blowing through us?

It's like the problem we had to prove there was a breeze coming from the fan. The moving pinwheel showed there was a breeze. Our actions prove that God's Holy Spirit is in us. He makes us kind, considerate, joyful, and patient, and will also give us many other good qualities.

Even though others can't see God, when they see these good qualities in us they will be seeing God at work.

Key Text

"But the fruit of the Spirit is love, joy, peace, patience, kindness, goodness, faithfulness, gentleness and self-control." (Gal. 5:22)

6

Be an Onion Christian

Objects Needed

A large onion, a dinner plate, and a knife.

Theme

Christians should not put up a false front but be the same through and through.

Presentation

There is something very interesting about an onion that I want to show you today. It's the fact that the onion is the same all the way through. I could take this onion and peel off a couple of layers and it would look just the same, except for being smaller. Let me do one layer and show you. (Peel a layer off.) See? We could keep peeling the onion and it would look the same, just smaller.

Perhaps an easier way to show you is to cut the onion in half like this. Now you can see the various rings of the onion. If you were to keep peeling the onion until you came to something that was different, you would end up peeling until there was nothing left. The onion is the same through and through.

We should be onion Christians. That may sound strange but this is what I mean: We should be Christ-like on the inside as well as on the outside. We should be his beautiful person through and through!

But I'm afraid that is not always the case. Have you ever met a person at school or in your neighborhood, smiled and said, "Hi," when inside you were thinking, "Boy, he (or she) is really dumb"? You see, we often try to pretend we are better people than we really are. Jesus called this being a hypocrite. Jesus wants us to be good not only on the outside but on the inside as well. We shouldn't go through life looking as though we really care for people and then be laughing at them or hating them in our thinking. God sees what we are thinking. We may be able to fool some of the people some of the time but not God. He knows what we are really thinking and feeling inside.

Let's be like an onion—the same through and through!

Key Text

"The LORD does not look at the things man looks at. Man looks at the outward appearance, but the LORD looks at the heart." (1 Sam. 16:7)

7

Twelve River Stones

Objects Needed

Twelve stones.

Theme

Don't forget what God has done for you.

Presentation

I want to tell you a short, exciting story from the Book of Joshua in the Old Testament. It will explain why I have these twelve stones.

After Moses died, Joshua became the leader of God's people. It was his job to lead the people into the new land God had promised them. But there was one problem: the Jordan River had to be crossed to get to this land and the river was flooded. How would they cross?

Well, God performed a miracle and made the river stop. The people were able to walk across on dry ground just like their parents and some of them had walked through the Red Sea forty years earlier with Moses. God was still with them. The parting of the river was a sure sign.

Before the waters came back, Joshua had a man from each of the twelve tribes take a stone from the riverbed and make a pile on the riverbank where they crossed. This served as a constant reminder of how God was with them and was helping them. After all, these stones had come from the bottom of the river that God had stopped!

I'm sure Joshua piled up those stones because he knew how quickly people forget about the things God has done for them.

What has God done for you? What are the things that make your life good? Can you share some of them? (If you're brave you can ask the children to offer some thoughts. Repeat them so the congregation can hear.)

Yes, God is good. Just as Joshua used some stones to help him and his people remember the good thing God had done, so we should work at always remembering what God has done for us. Don't forget what God has done for you!

Key Text

"He said to the Israelites, 'In the future when your descendants ask their fathers, 'What do these stones mean?' tell them, 'Israel crossed the Jordan on dry ground.' " (Josh. 4:21–22)

8

The Most Important Thing

Objects Needed

Can of spray paint, mothballs, and a padlock.

Theme

The only treasure that can always be kept is a relationship with Jesus.

Presentation

Can anyone tell me what I have here? That's right, this is a can of spray paint, these are mothballs, and this is a padlock. They may not seem to have a lot in common, but actually they do. Each of them is used to protect something. The paint covers objects made of metal and protects them from rust; the mothballs are put in a closet with clothes to protect them from moths; and the padlock is put on a door so that only the person with the key can unlock it—it protects the person's belongings from thieves.

But even with all this protection things still rust out, get eaten by moths, and are stolen. Everything we have, even our most precious and valuable possessions, will eventually wear out, rust out, or be stolen. Nothing lasts forever—that is, nothing except God and the things of God!

If we're looking for a treasure that will never disappoint us, a treasure that we can always have, that kind of treasure is a relationship with God. He will always be here. If we have faith in him and love for him we will always be his.

If we're going to spend time and effort at getting rich it shouldn't be for things that won't last, which is everything except God. He is the only thing that won't wear out, rust, or get stolen. The best goal we can have in life is to love and serve God more and more.

Key Text

"Do not store up for yourselves treasures on earth, where moth and rust destroy, and where thieves break in and steal. But store up for yourselves treasure in heaven, where moth and rust do not destroy, and where thieves do not break in and steal." (Matt. 6:19–20)

Paint

moth balls

lock

9

The Potential of a Peanut

Objects Needed

A peanut.

Theme

Each of us has the potential to be a great person for God.

Presentation

Today I want to talk about the common, ordinary peanut. Thanks to a wonderful man named George Washington Carver we know the peanut is very useful and valuable. It can be made into many other items besides peanut butter!

George Washington Carver was a black man who was born to a slave woman back in 1864. When he was ten years old he set out on his own without any money to try to make a good life for himself. He worked at many jobs and studied hard through grade school, high school, and then college.

He loved working with plants. He also wanted to help the poor farmers. He told them to plant peanuts because peanuts help the soil stay in better shape. Of course this meant that there would be more peanuts than people could possibly eat, so he set out to find new things to make from them.

He worked hard and found he could make artificial milk, cheese, butter, breakfast food, coffee, soap, flour, dyes, and insulating board—all from the common peanut! George Washington Carver eventually discovered more than three hundred things that can be made from peanuts.

The lesson we can learn from George Washington Carver and the peanut is that we can do amazing things with the ordinary things around us. You may think that other kids have a lot more in life than you do—more money, more toys, more brains, more strength. But God doesn't want us to complain about what we don't have. He wants us to use what we do have. If you don't have a lot of nice toys you can make your own out of things around the house. You'll be more proud of something you make than something you buy. If you do your very best at school that is more important than getting a good grade.

Ask God to help you do the most with what you have. Just as George Washington Carver made many marvelous things out of the peanut to help other people, so God can do many marvelous things with you. God can use your life to help others if you just let him.

Key Text

"Each one should use whatever gift he has received to serve others." (1 Peter 4:10)

10

The Greatest Trophy

Objects Needed

A trophy, a ribbon, and a certificate of achievement.

Theme

The best award we can receive is the praise of Jesus.

Presentation

I have some objects with me today that people work really hard to get. They are awards for some great accomplishment. As you can see, these awards come in different shapes and sizes. This one is a statue with some writing at the base. (Read.) It's called a trophy. It was given to a person who did an excellent job at _____ .

Here is a ribbon. Blue means first place and red usually means second place.

This certificate is designed to be hung on the wall. It describes the achievement of the person. (Read.)

It's wonderful to be able to win an award for working hard and doing something really great. But I want to talk about the most wonderful award of all. It's not a trophy, ribbon, or certificate. It's the award of having the praise of Jesus. As Christians, nothing should be more important and rewarding than knowing we are making Christ happy.

I know it's great to have a teacher, friend, parent, or coach say, "Good job." Just imagine how wonderful it will be to get to heaven and hear Jesus say, "Good job." That's what we have to look forward to!

Of course, it will take hard work and effort. Doing the right thing and pleasing Jesus every day is not easy. All he asks is that we do our best. He tells us he will help us.

Yes, it's great to win trophies, ribbons, and certificates for excelling in different things. But let's remember that the greatest award of all is knowing we are doing our best in pleasing Christ.

Key Text

"Well done, good and faithful servant!...Come and share in your master's happiness." (Matt. 25:21)

11

Unique and Useful

Objects Needed

Various tools such as a hammer, a screwdriver, a saw.

Theme

God has made each of us unique so that we can do the special work he wants us to do.

Presentation

Look at the different tools I brought with me today. Here's a hammer, used to pound nails. This is a screwdriver, used for turning screws into wood or metal. This saw cuts wood.

Do you think it would work to use a screwdriver to pound nails, a saw to tighten screws, or a hammer to saw wood? Of course not! Each tool is designed to do one job but not another. Does that mean the hammer isn't as good a tool because it can't cut wood like the saw? Does it mean that a screwdriver is a better tool simply because it can tighten a screw while a hammer or saw can't?

No, each tool is good in its own way and each tool has limits of what it can do well.

Did you know that each one of us is a tool of God's? That's right! He has made us with different gifts and abilities. Some of you may be good in music. Others can do well in sports. Still others are good in art or perhaps math.

Each of us needs to remember not to do two things when it comes to talents and abilities:

First, don't be jealous of someone else simply because he or she is better than you in something. You have your own talents and abilities. You may not always know what they are, but you have them.

Second, don't be proud that you can do some things better than other people. Remember that they will be better than you in some other way.

You may wonder if you can do anything at all. The answer is yes. Ask God to help you see what you are good at doing.

Yes, everyone is unique with different interests and abilities. The important point we all need to remember is that no one is better than anyone else, we're just different!

Key Text

"I remind you to fan into flame the gift of God, which is in you." (2 Tim. 1:6)

12

The Boat Rudder and the Tongue

Objects Needed

A toy boat with a rudder.

Theme

The tongue is like a boat rudder—it's small but has great power.

Presentation

Let's look closely at this boat. It can be steered in different directions because it has a small but important part that big boats have too—a rudder. Does anyone know where the rudder is? (Have someone show you.)

See how small it is compared to the rest of the boat. Actually, you can't even see it when the boat is going through the water. It's underneath, doing its job of steering the boat. When you turn it this way (turn rudder) it will go this way and when you turn the rudder this way the boat will turn the other way.

The Bible says our tongues are a lot like a boat's rudder—they're both small but they have tremendous power!

With your tongue you can make someone happy,

sad, or angry. Think about it. You can walk up to someone and tell that person something that will make him happy. You might say, ''You sure did a nice job on your project,'' or ''I like you as a friend.'' There are thousands of things you and I can say that will make people feel good. We can also say nasty things such as, ''You're so short,'' or ''Boy, that was a dumb thing to do.'' Such things make other people sad.

God wants you to use that little thing called the tongue in a beautiful, helpful way.

Remember, the tongue may be small just like the rudder of a boat is small. But, like the boat rudder, the tongue has tremendous power. Use it to steer you to say good things to people.

Key Text

''Or take ships as an example. Although they are so large and are driven by strong winds, they are steered by a very small rudder wherever the pilot wants to go. Likewise the tongue is a small part of the body, but it makes great boasts.'' (James 3:4–5)

13

Run the Race

Objects Needed

A pair of running shoes or tennis shoes.

Theme

Being a Christian is like running a race; it takes concentrated effort.

Presentation

How many of you have ever run in a race? I see that some of you have. Running is very popular these days. There always seems to be someone running alongside the road.

Some of the runners we see are preparing for a race. A few are preparing for the most grueling race of all, the marathon. That's over twenty miles long!

Most runners wear special shoes like these, called running shoes. They are built to make running as easy as possible, though it still takes tremendous effort, concentration, and energy.

The apostle Paul says that living life to please Jesus is a lot like running a race. The runner never looks back over his shoulder, otherwise he might run into something or stumble. He also will lose a little speed and someone else might get out ahead of him. As

Christians we should remember that Jesus has forgiven our sins, we don't have to keep thinking guilty
thoughts about them. It does no good to say, "I wish I
would have done this or that differently." It's over and
done with.

The good runner keeps looking forward toward the
finish line. That's where he focuses his attention. As
Christians we should also be looking toward the finish
line. Our goal is to live close to Jesus and doing things his
way. There is no better purpose you and I can have in life
than to want to grow close to Jesus and to please him!

The runner also has to work hard at running the
race. It's not easy! Have you ever noticed how runners
huff and puff and sweat? They really put effort into
running. You and I must also put a great deal of effort
into our Christian lives. How many of you find it hard
to do the good and Christ-like things in life? Yes, I do
too. It takes concentrated effort to keep putting Jesus
first in life and trying to do things the way he wants us
to. But it's worth it for we will be closer to Jesus and
will be happy knowing we have pleased him. We will
feel like we are winning the race of life!

So let these running shoes remind you that living
the Christian life is like running an exciting race. Don't
look back on the sins God has already forgiven; keep
looking at Jesus and work hard at being the person he
wants you to be. You will be a winner!

Key Text

"But one thing I do: Forgetting what is behind and
straining toward what is ahead, I press on toward the
goal to win the prize for which God has called me
heavenward in Christ Jesus." (Phil. 3:13–14)

14

Prayer Lets Blessings Flow

Objects Needed

A large-capacity coffee maker with a faucet; a drinking glass.

Preparation

Put some water in the coffee maker.

Theme

Prayer unleashes God's goodness into our lives.

Presentation

A faucet is an interesting device. It's quite amazing. You simply go up to it, turn it on, and water comes out. I'm sure you don't think there's much to get excited about here, but people have not always had such an easy way to get water. I imagine some of your grandparents or great grandparents can remember a time long ago when they did not have running water. They had to go out to a well, pump by hand, and carry the water back to the house. The only way they had running water was if they ran with the bucket.

Now all we have to do is turn on a faucet like this and water comes out.

Today I want us to think of prayer as a faucet. When

we pray we open up the flow of God's goodness into our lives. When we don't pray some of God's goodness stays stored up.

God has so much he wants to give to people and do for them; he is the richest and most powerful Being in the whole universe! But God has set things up in such a way that he wants us, his people, to have a part in unleashing his powerful help and goodness. He wants us to pray.

Of course God is not exactly like a faucet. God can think about whether or not something we pray for is really the best thing so sometimes he gives us a "no" answer.

Yet, the fact is, we miss out on a great deal of God's goodness and help in life simply because we don't ask for it.

Pray and ask God to help you in different ways. Pray for your family, friends, the church, and others you think of. Your prayers are like turning on a faucet. Your prayers will help God's goodness to flow into your life and the lives of those you love.

Key Text

"Ask and it will be given to you....For everyone who asks receives." (Matt. 7:7–8)

15

Let Christ Remake You

Objects Needed

A piece of typing paper, two thick books, a drinking glass, and a tray.

Preparation

Have the two books placed approximately six inches apart on the tray.

Theme

God can make us stronger and more useful.

Presentation

Let's pretend these two books are two cliffs and we are going to build a bridge between them. The only thing we have with which to make our bridge is this piece of paper. I wonder how good a bridge it will make? We'll lay it across the two books, our pretend cliffs. Let's put some weight on it to see if our bridge is very strong. It sags when we put this glass on it. I don't think it will make a very good bridge, do you?

But wait a minute—I think I can make the piece of paper into a much stronger bridge. I'll take it and fold it back and forth, like you do when making a fan (make narrow folds, about one-half inch in width).

There. Now that we've made it into what's called a corrugated shape we'll place it across the two books and try it again. Now I'll put the glass on our bridge (do this gently so that the glass sets on as many folds as possible).

See! It can support the glass. We made a strong bridge after all.

There's nothing magical about it. It's just that a piece of paper that's folded back and forth is stronger than a flat piece of paper.

You and I can be stronger and more useful, like our pretend bridge, if we let God mold, fold, and make us into more of the person he wants us to be.

Let God get close to you. Let him come and live inside of you. He will do even more amazing things than we have done with this paper. He will help make you into a more beautiful and useful person. Let God control how you think, talk, and act. Pray each day, "Dear Jesus, help me to be the person you want me to be."

Just as I folded and molded this piece of paper into something stronger and more useful, so let God get to you and fold and mold you into being his better person.

Key Text

"Offer yourselves to God." (Rom. 6:13)

16

Put God in Charge

Objects Needed

A toy airplane.

Theme

Just as we let a pilot fly the plane in which we ride, so we should let the Lord control our lives.

Presentation

How many of you have ever flown in an airplane? I have too and it's a lot of fun. Some of you who have flown may have glanced into the cockpit when you boarded the plane and perhaps those of you who haven't flown have seen a cockpit in pictures or on television. Does it have about the same number of gauges, dials, switches, and controls as a car has? No! It has many, many more. A cockpit is filled with controls.

When it's time to take off, the pilot starts the engines by turning and flipping just the right switches. He checks out a great many dials as well. Finally, he moves the plane faster and faster along the runway and takes off (make toy plane soar). He then flies it until you reach your destination and then lands it safely once again.

How many of you would like to fly a plane? So

would I. I think it would be really exciting. But I never do and neither do you when you take a plane on a trip. That's because we don't know how to fly a plane. It would be really dumb for us to try.

Do you know who is the only one who really knows absolutely everything about life and living? Of course, it's the Lord! He invented this thing we call life. He knows best how we ought to live it. The smart thing is to let him be in charge of "piloting" our lives. Too many people try to run their lives their own way and they end up ruining them. God is the only one who has all that it takes to run life right, just as only the pilot can fly a plane.

You and I need to let Jesus, God's Son, be the pilot of our lives. If you have never done it before, ask Jesus to be the one to run your life. Tell him you want to do everything his way, that he can be in charge. Just as it's real smart to let a pilot fly the plane, so it is smart to let Jesus be the one to run and rule your life so that it turns out good.

Key Text

"He [Jesus] became the source of eternal salvation for all who obey him." (Heb. 5:9)

17

Different Views

Objects Needed

Two copies of a sketch that can look either like a vase or two faces.

Preparation

On a piece of paper or cardboard draw this type of design. Draw a similar one on a second piece of paper or cardboard.

Theme

Jesus wants us to love and respect those who may have a different point of view from our own.

Presentation

What do you see when you look at this drawing? Some people see a vase while others see two faces. How many of you first saw a vase? How many of you first saw two faces?

You know, it's amazing how angry people can get at each other simply because they don't see something the same way. But it's very selfish to want others to see things exactly as we see them. The other person may not be any more right or wrong than we are. Because people are different they see things differently and that's OK.

I'll take one drawing and show you that it's a vase. All I have to do is draw two lines.

Now I'll take the other drawing and show you it can also be two faces. All I need to add is two dots.

Both opinions are right in this case. It would have been silly to get angry at the other person.

You will disagree with many people in your life. You may feel strongly they are wrong and you are right. Just remember, the loving thing to do is to love and accept them even though you don't agree. That's what Jesus would want us to do.

Key Text

"Love is patient, love is kind. It does not envy, it does not boast, it is not proud. It is not rude, it is not self-seeking, it is not easily angered, it keeps no record of wrongs." (1 Cor. 13:4–5)

18

Different and Unique

Objects Needed

A selection of different balls (golf ball, basketball, baseball, tennis ball, croquet ball, bowling ball).

Theme

Just as different balls are designed to be played in different games, so God has designed everyone differently so as to accomplish his unique calling for each person.

Presentation

This is quite a collection of balls I have here. Each one is really different from the others. (Allow them to name each ball before you discuss it.)

This golf ball is hard and has hundreds of little indentations in it. It's designed to fly great distances through the air after being hit very hard with a golf club.

But imagine trying to use a golf ball to play basketball. Dribbling down the floor to shoot a basket would be real difficult. Which ball do you need to play basketball?

Here's a wooden croquet ball. To play croquet you are supposed to hit this ball with a wooden mallet. What if you tried to play golf with it? I wonder how bent up your golf club would be after hitting it? No, a croquet ball is meant to be used only with a mallet.

One more. Here's a bowling ball. Can you imagine playing basketball with it? How about trying to bowl with a golf ball? Ridiculous, isn't it?

Just as different balls have been designed for different purposes, so you and I have been made by God to do specific things for him.

Some of you are good at music while others are good at a certain sport. Still others are good at math. Each of you also has different interests, so you concentrate and spend your time on different things. You also are all built differently. Some people are made tall, some short, some thin, some heavier.

Just as it is ridiculous to compare a golf ball to a bowling ball or a basketball to a croquet ball, so it is ridiculous and unfair to compare people to each other. We shouldn't put down others or ourselves just because we are different from one another.

God has made each one of you to do his own good purpose in a special way. Don't try to be somebody else. Don't try to make others be like you. Just be the best YOU you can be and let the other person do the same! Be yourself but be the best self you can be!

Key Text

"We have different gifts, according to the grace given us." (Rom. 12:6)

19

Room for Jesus

Objects Needed

A closed box with the word *Jesus* written on it, a collection of things important to children (doll, toy truck, big storybook, etc.), and a container that is small enough to be overflowing when all of the above items are placed inside.

Theme

We shouldn't let life get so crowded with ''things'' that we have no room for Jesus.

Presentation

Do I have a collection of items for you today! As I pull them out of the paper bag I'll put them into the basket (or whatever container you have).

Let's see. First, here's a doll, then we have a big storybook. We also have a toy truck and a radio. We can't leave out food so here's a box of cereal. How about a football? Oh, yes, there's one more; this box will stand for Jesus.

It looks like we have trouble here. Not all the things fit into our basket and there certainly is no room for Jesus.

Did you know that this is exactly what can happen in our lives? We can be so busy with all the other interesting, fun, and important things that we don't have much room for Jesus. He can easily get crowded out.

We can get so busy and interested in other things that we don't have time to talk to Jesus in prayer, read the Bible, go to church, or simply take time to think about him and how wonderful he is.

It's not that these other things are bad; they aren't. It's just that we can become so involved and interested in everything else that we forget about Jesus. That's when these other things become bad.

God wants you and me to have his good gifts, such as the items in the basket here today. But he also wants us to leave room for Jesus. In fact, Jesus wants to be the most important part of our lives!

So, when your life gets so busy and exciting with all kinds of things to do, places to go, and things to play with, stop and think about Jesus. Send a prayer up to him and say something like this, "Jesus, I thank you for all these fun things I can do and can have, but I want you to know that you are the most important to me." He would appreciate that.

Let's make certain we have enough room in our lives for Jesus.

Key Text

"No one can serve two masters. Either he will hate the one and love the other, or he will be devoted to the one and despise the other. You cannot serve both God and Money [things]." (Matt. 6:24)

20

Depending on God

Objects Needed

Goldfish (or other fish) in bowl.

Theme

Just as a pet owner takes care of his pet, so God takes care of us.

Presentation

How many of you have a pet at home? (Allow them to share what kind of pets they have.) Many people have pets. Today I have with me a pet goldfish.

Goldfish are fun pets. You can relax and be entertained simply by the way they swim so gracefully.

But if you are going to have a pet goldfish, there are certain things you must do. You must feed it every day, change its water frequently, and watch to see that it is healthy. There are also some things you can't do with a goldfish. You can't take it for a walk, can you! Or teach it tricks! You have to know the limitations of your pet. I hope that every one of you who has a pet knows what you should and shouldn't do for it. That way your pet will stay happy and healthy.

Did you know that God wants to take much better care of us than even the best pet owner does of his pet?

You and I are God's people; he made us so that if we follow him he will take good care of us. God will give us the food, clothing, and roof over our heads that we need. He will also provide us with family and friends. He will always help us in tough situations. Nothing has to get us down; God will always be there to help.

There is a very big difference between us taking care of our pets and God taking care of us. Most of our pets are in cages or aquariums or on chains, or locked in the house or in the yard. God doesn't *force* us to be his. We can run away from him if we want. It's sad for God and for us if we do this. God wants us to stay with him, believe in him, and follow him. Be God's person and let him care for you.

Key Text

"Know that the LORD is God. It is he who made us, and we are his; we are his people, the sheep of his pasture." (Ps. 100:3)

21

God Is Here

Objects Needed

A portable radio.

Theme

We may not be able to see God but nevertheless he is right here with us.

Presentation

Do you see anything floating around in the air? Except for a few specks of dust, I don't. It looks to me like there is really nothing much at all in the air around us.

But that's not true! This portable radio will prove that there's more in the air than we can see. When I turn it on like this and turn the tuning dial what happens? You hear a radio program. Where did it come from? The radio's antenna pulled in the radio waves that are found right around it, right around us. Isn't that amazing! Around us right now are the radio waves this radio is picking up. We don't see them, hear them, taste them, or feel them but they are there nevertheless.

The Bible says that God is spirit. One of the things about something that is spirit is that you can't see it! Like the radio waves, God is all around us right this moment even though we can't see him. Just as we need a radio to pick up radio waves so that we might hear them, so we need to use something that can help us feel that God is right with us. It's not any kind of an instrument. It's an attitude. It's called faith. The way you and I can feel God's presence in our lives is by faith—believing that he is here with us even though we don't see him. God does not make himself magically appear so that people have to believe in him. He wants people like you and me to believe in him because we want to.

If we want to feel God close by we must always believe he is there. We must love him, depend on him, try to please him as he watches us, and talk to him often. Then he will become more and more real to us.

Yes, there are radio waves in the air even though we can't see them. With the help of a radio we know they are there. And yes, God is right here with us now even though we can't see him. With the help of faith we can know he is here.

Key Text

"Now faith is being sure of what we hope for and certain of what we do not see." (Heb. 11:1)

22

Love Binds Us Together

Objects Needed
Tape, glue, stapler, and a bolt.

Theme
It is love for each other that helps us to stay close.

Presentation
I would like for you to discover what this tape, glue, stapler, and bolt have in common. Think about it. (Allow them to answer.) That's right! They are all used to hold things together. Most of you probably have tape and glue in your desk at school or in your room. You may also have a stapler of your own, or perhaps your teacher or parents do. Your father probably has a jar of bolts in the garage that he uses to hold metal or wooden objects together.

Almost everything we have has to be held together by something. Can you name a few of them? There is something else that needs to be held together as well and that is people. We need to be close to people. If we are not, life becomes very sad and lonely. We need to be close to our family, to our friends, and to our fellow church people—plus many others. Let me tell you what holds people together better than anything else:

love! Love is the best tape, the best glue, the best staple, the best bolt that you can find to keep you close to people.

There are other things that we sometimes think keep us close to others but they don't work as well as love. You may think that it's because you live on the same street that you are friends with a certain person, but if that is all that makes you friends it will be over with the first time you have a serious fight. Sometimes we think we are close friends with someone because we like the same sport or the same games but this usually doesn't last either. Even living in the same house with your family will not automatically make you close to them. In every case what we really need is love for that person.

No matter what you like doing with someone close to you, just remember that to love that person is the most important thing of all. Love will be the tape, the glue, the staple, the bolt that holds your friendship together.

Key Text

"A friend loves at all times." (Prov. 17:17)

23

Show Your Love for Jesus

Objects Needed

A Greek New Testament (or anything written in a foreign language).

Theme

We need to show people that we love Jesus in a way they can understand.

Presentation

I have a New Testament with me today. Would someone please read the first line at the top of this page? (Hand it to an older child who can read and whom you won't embarrass.) What's the matter? Why can't you read a verse out of the New Testament? Actually, I'm teasing you because I doubt if many people here could read it themselves; it's the New Testament but it's the Greek New Testament. Unless you know how to read Greek it will be impossible for you to understand anything of God's Word written here. We want and need God's Word written in a way that we can understand it; we need it in English!

Did you know that some of your friends who don't love Jesus have a hard time understanding what being a Christian is all about? They see church buildings and perhaps a Bible lying around but that doesn't explain much about being a Christian. They may even have gone to a church service but it was all so different and unusual to them that they really didn't understand what it was all about.

They don't know that being a Christian means we are loved and forgiven by Jesus and that we love him back and try to live our lives to please him. They don't understand what being a Christian means just like you don't understand this Greek New Testament when it talks about Jesus.

This Greek New Testament had to be translated into English for you to understand it. You must translate what it means to be a Christian into a form that those who don't love Jesus will understand. Let me tell you very simply the way to show others what being a Christian is all about.

With the help of Jesus try in every situation to do what is right, good, and fair. This means you won't cheat on a test even though other students are and you think you can get away with it. It means that you will be kind to someone who doesn't have any friends. It means you share your toys with others. You should also quickly forgive those who do wrong to you.

The most important thing about being a Christian witness for others is to show them Christian love. If they ask, you can tell them you are tying to do the right thing because Jesus loves you and you love him and want to please him. This is the way they will begin to understand what it means to be a Christian. After all, everyone understands love.

Key Text

"A new command I give you: Love one another. As I have loved you, so you must love one another. All men will know that you are my disciples if you love one another." (John 13:34–35)

24

God's Instructions and Guarantees

Objects Needed

Two large manila envelopes. In one are several instruction books and guarantees for household appliances. In the second envelope is a Bible.

Theme

The Bible is God's book of instructions and guarantees for our lives.

Presentation

I'd like you to see what I have in this envelope. Here's an instruction manual for our refrigerator and another for our lawnmower. They are directions from the manufacturers, the people who made the machines, on how to keep the lawnmower and refrigerator working well. It would be silly to spend a lot of money to buy something and then ruin it simply because you didn't read the instructions.

Here is a guarantee for our electric water heater. A guarantee is a promise by the company that built the heater. They promise it will work. They are so sure that it will work that they will fix it free if it doesn't.

As you can see, this envelope is important to me because it contains the instructions and guarantees for the things I own.

I have another envelope here that also contains many instructions and guarantees. It's the Bible.

The Bible is God's book of instructions for us. He thought us up. He made us. You might say he is our manufacturer. Because he made us and this marvelous thing called life, he knows best how we ought to live it. When you and I read God's Word or hear it taught and we obey it, we will find that life is what it should be.

The Bible also has many promises or guarantees in it. God promises to do many wonderful things if we follow his plan for us. He promises to forgive us, help us, stay with us, and take us to heaven someday, along with many, many other wonderful promises.

As you live your life always try to read, listen to, and obey God's Word, the Bible. It's filled with instructions and guarantees that can make life good.

Key Text

"Your word is a lamp to my feet and a light for my path." (Ps. 119:105)

25

Slow Growth

Objects Needed

Packet of garden seeds, tray, dirt, pot, water.

Theme

People change and grow slowly so we need to have patience with them.

Presentation

You know, it's fun to grow plants. In fact, we're going to grow some plants right now. First, I'll fill this flower pot with dirt. Now we poke some holes in the soil, put in the seeds, and cover them up. Good. Now we'll add some water—after all, plants need water. That should do it. They ought to grow. Let's sit back and watch them come up. (Stare at the pot for a few moments.) We did everything properly. Why aren't the plants growing? (Let kids answer.) That's right! It takes time. By next Sunday they should be up but not much sooner. Plants take time to grow.

You take time to grow as well. You are taller and stronger than you were a year ago but it didn't happen overnight. It took a year to grow that much.

People grow another way as well. They grow spiritually. What I mean by that is that people, like you and me, can grow closer to God and can grow to be more Christ-like. We can become less selfish and more loving, less sour and more joyful; and the list could go on and on.

The problem is that we often get impatient with each other. Perhaps you can think of a Christian friend, brothers or sisters, or even parents with whom you get aggravated occasionally. When a person does things that you feel aren't right how should you react? I believe you should react the same way we do to these newly planted seeds: have patience! Most things grow slowly and that includes Christians as well as seeds.

So be patient with each other. Forgive each other. It's going to take time for all of us to grow and become more like Jesus.

Key Text

"Don't grumble against each other." (James 5:9)

26

A Mirror or Window Christian?

Objects Needed

A small mirror and a piece of glass.

Theme

We shouldn't always be thinking of ourselves but should think more about the needs of others.

Presentation

Here are two objects that are both made from glass. Yet they are quite different. Can anyone tell me what the difference is? One is used as a window and the other is used as a mirror.

Windows are used to look through so that you can see other things. Mirrors are for looking at yourself.

God doesn't want us to always be thinking about ourselves but to be thinking more about other people. Guess which he would rather we be like—the mirror or the window? That's right, the window. God wants us to spend more time looking out for others than looking out for ourselves.

Doing it God's way actually makes life more enjoyable. When you and I spend more time thinking about what other people need and less time about our own wants and needs, we become happier people.

Imagine living in a house where all the windows have been turned into mirrors. Think about it. How would you like living there? You wouldn't be able to see outside. You wouldn't see the sun, the trees, the clouds, your friends walking by, or anything else. It would also make your house as dark as it is at night because no light can get through a mirror.

The same thing happens when you and I think mainly about ourselves. Life gets gloomy for us. We stop seeing the beautiful things around us and the exciting way we could help other people. We only see ourselves. It's like living in a house where all the windows have been replaced with mirrors.

Let's be more the person God wants us to be. Let's think more about other people and less about ourselves. May our eyes be more like a window that can see the world around us and less like the mirror that only lets us see ourselves. Be a window Christian!

Key Text

"Each of you should look not only to your own interests, but also to the interests of others." (Phil. 2:4)

27

Don't Be Tricked

Objects Needed

A mask of some kind.

Theme

Satan is the ultimate deceiver and makes evil appear to be good.

Presentation

Children wear one of these around Halloween. Adults might wear one if they go to a costume party. You might wear one when pretending with a friend.

A mask can be fun to play with. You can pretend to be somebody else. See, when I put this mask in front of my face I look like a different character. I may even frighten small children by wearing this (or, ''by wearing a scary mask''). But you know that it is really me underneath, don't you? Wearing the mask does not change who I really am.

There is someone else who wears masks and that is Satan. He is a master at disguises. His purpose in life is to try to trick people into believing that doing what he wants is going to be good and fun when it is not. He wants to keep us from doing things God's good way and do it his evil way instead.

Satan can get us to think that cheating on a test at school will be easier than studying for it. He will get us to believe that saying or doing something nasty to someone else is "cool." He makes us think that disobeying our parents is more fun than obeying them.

Doing things Satan's way looks so good at the time. But he is deceiving us, fooling us. Satan's way always ends up turning out bad. We end up getting caught, hurting our friends, or feeling miserable afterwards about what we have done. This is why Satan is called the great deceiver. He makes things look good when they are bad.

The next time you get to thinking about doing something that you know is wrong but that looks fun and easy, or will help you be accepted by your friends, stop and think about whether it might be sin in disguise. Satan may be taking something bad and putting a nice mask on it so it looks good. If you realize it is Satan trying to trick you, don't let him fool you! Tell him to get away from you.

Satan wants to trick you into doing what is bad so that you end up hurting yourself, others, and God. God's way may be more difficult at the time, but in the end it will be much better!

Key Text

"Satan himself masquerades as an angel of light." (2 Cor. 11:14)

28

God's Goodness Is Like Yeast

Objects Needed

A packet of yeast and a slice of bread.

Theme

God's goodness (his kingdom) works slowly but it works surely, influencing all of life.

Presentation

I have brought a very common object with me today. It's a food I suspect most of you eat at least once a day. It's a slice of bread. I want to show you something about this slice of bread. Look closely. Do you see all the little holes and air pockets in it? Bread is just full of these. It's all of these holes that make the bread light and fluffy.

Now I want to show you what puts those holes and air pockets into a loaf when it is baked. It's this—a substance called yeast. When the baker mixes up his bread dough he always puts in some yeast. When the yeast gets warm inside the loaf of bread it starts producing gas that forms bubbles inside the loaf. This makes the loaf rise and become nice and fluffy. Without yeast the loaf of bread would be so small, heavy, and hard that you would hardly be able to eat it.

Yeast almost seems like a secret substance because it works so quietly that you don't notice it. You can't see the bread dough rising and getting bigger because it happens so slowly. When you look back at it later, however, you see that it really has risen.

Jesus says that God's kingdom is like yeast. God's kingdom is the good influence and control he has. It's like yeast in that it influences people's lives slowly and quietly. You don't often find out about the things God is doing when you read the paper or watch the news on television, do you? But God is there, working.

God is also willing to do his good things in your life and mine if we let him. He can help you be a better student and friend. He can also help you get along better with your family so that your life at home is happier. In many different ways God wants to use you to make life better. You probably won't get your name in the paper or on TV for being a good Christian but that doesn't matter; you'll be pleasing God and helping the people and situations around you.

In this way you will be a lot like yeast, having a quiet but good influence on others. That's the way the kingdom of God works, too!

Key Text

"He told them still another parable: 'The kingdom of heaven is like yeast that a woman took and mixed into a large amount of flour until it worked all through the dough.' " (Matt. 13:33)

29

Be a Sample for Jesus

Objects Needed

A sample-size package of some product.

Theme

We can be a small sample of what Jesus is like to those around us.

Presentation

You can buy most objects at the store in different size containers; some are big and some are small.

See how tiny this bottle of shampoo is (or whatever product it is)? It is called a sample size. It cost very little. Sometimes companies actually give samples like this away.

Sample sizes are made by many different companies so that you will try their product. They figure that if you have to pay only a few cents for a sample or are given one free, then maybe you will try their product. If you like the product there is a good chance you will go out and buy a bigger container of it at the regular price.

Did you know that you too can be a sample? You can be a sample for Jesus. If you have asked Jesus to come into your heart and if you want to please him, you are a Christian. But not all the people around you are

Christians. They may not know what a real Christian is like. They may think that being a Christian is no fun. But if they get to know you they will begin to see Jesus living in you. They will see that being a Christian is a great thing to do after all. You are a sample to them!

Even if they don't go to church, read the Bible, or pray, if they know you as a friend they will still be learning a lot about Jesus. They may decide to love and follow Jesus like you.

This sample-size bottle may get me to buy the regular size, and keep buying it. Will you be a sample size of Jesus so that others will want to know him and love him like you do?

Key Text

"But you will receive power when the Holy Spirit comes on you; and you will be my witnesses in Jerusalem, and in all Judea and Samaria, and to the ends of the earth." (Acts 1:8)

30

Let Go of Sin

Objects Needed

A glass jar with a neck small enough so that a child can put his hand in but can't pull it out when a fist is made, and a cookie.

Theme

It's wrong to hold on to things that are sinful. We should let go of them.

Presentation

I am going to show you how to catch a monkey! This is actually a method used in the jungle for catching wild monkeys.

A jar or vase with just the right-size neck is used. Then some food that monkeys love is placed inside the jar. Because we are going to use one of you to demonstrate how it works, we'll use a food people like: a cookie. I'll drop it into the jar like this. Now, will one of you try to get the cookie out?

If your hand is the right size it's not so hard getting it in but notice how you can't pull your hand out when holding the cookie.

For catching monkeys the jar is tied down with a rope. The monkey grabs hold of the food in the jar and finds it can't get its hand out. Of course it could release the food and pull its hand right out, but it won't. It doesn't want to let go of the food. The hunters simply walk up and capture the stubborn monkey.

The captured monkeys could have had their freedom if they would only have been willing to let go of the food in the jar.

Did you know that people get into the same kind of trouble? Oh, we don't put our hands into jars and stubbornly refuse to let go, but we do keep holding on to things that are bad for us.

Let's list some things that we like to do even though they get us into trouble. Do you enjoy punching someone back when he punches you? Do you like to talk back nasty to people when they have talked nasty to you? Do you play when you should be doing your homework? Do you think about fun things you want to do while your Sunday school teacher is talking? We could go on and on.

So often, doing something wrong or bad looks like fun at the time and so we go ahead and do it. Then we get caught and get into trouble, or we end up doing it again and again until we realize we can't seem to stop doing it.

Sin is like that food in the jar for the monkey; if you hold on to it and don't let go it will have you captured. Who wants to be captured by Satan and his sin? This is what we ought to do instead: The next time you realize you are enjoying doing something wrong, think of the monkey with his hand in the jar getting caught because he won't let go. Let go of doing the bad thing you want to do. Get away from doing that sinful thing and you will still be a free person able to live your life to please God.

Key Text

"Submit yourselves, then, to God. Resist the devil, and he will flee from you." (James 4:7)

31

On the Rock or Sand

Objects Needed

Two small objects representing houses (could be made from a wooden building block with a folded piece of paper for a roof), a flat rock, sand, a tray, and a pitcher of water.

Preparation

Although this object lesson takes a little more preparation, the children will never forget its graphic depiction of this parable of our Lord's. Place the rock on the tray and cover it over with sand, making certain only a thin layer of sand is on top of the rock. Place one of the houses on the rock. Build a mound of equal size out of sand next to the first house, leaving a narrow valley between. Place the second house on this mound. Pour the water into the valley between the houses, making certain you undermine the house on the sand so it tumbles down. The pouring water should also be moved over so that it washes away the sand covering the rock. Don't pour water directly on the houses. Practice this procedure at least once. It is not as difficult as it sounds and the effect is worth the extra preparation.

Theme

It is with Christ and his Word that we survive the tough times in life.

Presentation

Jesus told a story about two houses and what happened to each one during a storm. Here's the story.

Once there were two houses. One had been built on the rock. It's not easy to build on rock because it is difficult to make holes for the foundation. The other house was built on the sand. Its owner had a much easier time building it because sand is easy to dig in. Both houses looked good.

But then the storm came with its flood (begin pouring the water). The rains kept beating against the earth and the waters kept rising. The house on the rock stood firm because rock doesn't wash away. But the house built on the sand ended up tumbling into the flooded waters and being destroyed because the sand underneath it gave way.

Jesus says our lives can be either like the house on the rock or the house on the sand. He says that when we love him, depend on him, and obey his Word we are doing the right thing. We are like the house on the rock and will be OK. But if we don't come to Jesus and don't depend on him or obey him we are being foolish. When the tough times come our way we won't be able to take them. We'll be all washed up!

Make sure you are like the house on the rock. Depend on the one person in the universe who is bigger and stronger than a huge rock, Jesus. Stay with him and you will be OK!

Key Text

"Therefore everyone who hears these words of mine and puts them into practice is like a wise man who built his house on the rock." (Matt. 7:24)

32

Outer Labels

Objects Needed

Can of corn (or other product), piece of paper cut to label size, marking pen, tape, banana with sticker, apple.

Theme

Neither the clothes we wear, the size of our home, the toys we can afford, nor the grades we get at school indicate our value as a person. It's what's inside that counts.

Presentation

Here is a can of corn. Let's pretend I don't like corn. Instead, I'd rather have carrots. I'll just take this piece of paper and make a new label. I'm writing "carrots" on it. Now I'll wrap it around the can and fasten it with some tape. Now I have a can of carrots, right? (You may want to open the can at this point.) Wrong! It doesn't matter what label I put on the can, it still will be corn. It's what's inside that counts.

The same thing is true with this banana and apple. I can take this banana label off the banana and put it on the apple (bite into the apple or slice it up and distribute), but it still tastes like an apple, even with the banana label. It's what's inside that counts.

We people have many different labels. Some of you

are boys and some are girls, but either way you are a person whom God loves. Some kids are smart in school and some are not so smart; either way, you can be a beautiful person inside. Some kids have fancy clothes in the latest styles while other kids' parents can't afford that for them. But do you know what? God doesn't care. It's what's in your heart that counts. Some kids are tall while others are short; some are skinny while others are heavy. God doesn't look at this. He looks at the real us inside.

What makes you or me a beautiful, successful person in the eyes of God is what's inside. If you and I love Jesus, have asked forgiveness for our sins, and decide to live our lives to please him, this is what is most important.

Outer labels of clothes, toys, grades, or how our bodies look aren't the most important part of us. It's what's inside that counts.

Key Text

"The LORD does not look at the things man looks at. Man looks at the outward appearance, but the LORD looks at the heart." (1 Sam. 16:7)

33

Better than Butterflies

Objects Needed

A cocoon or a picture of one.

Theme

Being alive with Jesus in heaven after we die is a far greater miracle than the butterfly emerging from its cocoon.

Presentation

Do you know what this object is that I'm holding in my hand? Yes, a cocoon. Some time ago a caterpillar was crawling along the ground and felt the urge to find a protected spot. He then began the process of spinning this cocoon around himself. If we were to open this up right now we would not see what appears to be a living creature but a lifeless blob. It lies in here motionless, as though it were dead.

What is happening is one of the miracles of God's creation. A process called metamorphosis is taking place. I know metamorphosis seems like a big fancy word but all it means is change. A change is taking place. When springtime comes this cocoon will break open and out will come a beautiful butterfly. What looked like something dead has actually come to life in a far more beautiful form than before.

When a Christian dies it is similar to the experience of the butterfly except far better and more amazing. It seems like the body of the person lying in the casket is dead and can't move, think, or talk. That body can't, but the real person in that body, the soul, is already alive and with Jesus in heaven. He is experiencing the beautiful things of heaven and is especially enjoying a wonderful relationship with God. Someday, when Jesus comes back to earth, he will transform that person's body, and all other Christians' bodies, into beautiful new resurrection bodies! We will be far more beautiful than any butterfly. We will have a new resurrection body just like Jesus did after he was raised from the dead.

Just remember that when a Christian dies it's a little like the caterpillar going into a cocoon. But the same God who performs the miracle of having new life coming out of that seemingly lifeless cocoon will also give new life to the Christian who has died. For the person who loves Jesus death is not the end but just the beginning of a marvelous new life forever in his presence!

Key Text

Jesus said..., "I am the resurrection and the life. He who believes in me will live, even though he dies." (John 11:25)

34

A Limit to Temptations

Objects Needed

An electrical fuse for a house.

Theme

God will never allow us to be tempted above that which we are able to bear.

Presentation

This object is called a fuse. It may not look very interesting. I don't think any of you would care to go out and spend your allowance on buying one. Yet it is very important that all homes have some of these or something like it called a circuit breaker. A fuse can keep a house from burning down; that's how important it can be!

All of our homes have electrical wires running through the walls to the various switches, lights, and outlets. These wires carry the electricity that allows our lights to burn bright and our appliances to run.

But sometimes we run too many appliances and gadgets from the same circuit (the same wire). This could cause the wire in the walls to get so hot that it could start the walls on fire. Don't worry though. This won't happen because you have fuses some place in your house in a box called the electrical box. Perhaps your mom or dad could show you where it's located. The fuse will stop the flow of electricity when it has reached the point where it might cause damage. Fuses are wonderful little devices; they never let more electricity go through your home's wiring than is safe.

Did you know that God acts something like an electrical fuse with us? That's right. He will never allow a temptation to come our way that is too great for us to handle. All of us face the temptation to do something wrong, don't we? You want to give in and do what is wrong, and sometimes you can hardly stand it, but remember: Jesus will never let such a strong temptation come your way that you would just have to give in to it. No! God would stop such a temptation. Whenever you are tempted to do wrong you can be certain that the Lord knows you can overcome it, otherwise he wouldn't have let it come to you. You will never face a temptation that you just can't resist. God won't let that happen.

Key Text

"No temptation has seized you except what is common to man. And God is faithful; he will not let you be tempted beyond what you can bear. But when you are tempted, he will also provide a way out so that you can stand up under it." (1 Cor. 10:13)

35

How Creative God Is!

Objects Needed

Several kinds of seeds from wild plants that illustrate the different methods seeds use to travel to a new location—for instance, maple (spins through air), milkweed or cottonwood (floats through air), cocklebur (sticks to animals or people).

Theme

Just as God uses a variety of ways for plant seeds to find a new location in which to grow, so God has created each one of us different from others so that we might fulfill our unique calling in life.

Presentation

We have such a creative God! Let me show you just a few of the ways God gets his plant seeds spread all over. In our gardens we carry the seeds around and plant them. In the wild there are no people to do this so God has used his creative powers to produce different seeds like these I've brought with me.

Here's a maple seed from a maple tree. When you drop it like this (drop the seed) it spins around and around like a helicopter. The wind carries the spinning seed to a new location.

This seed is called a cocklebur. Have any of you ever had one of these stick to your jeans or socks while you were hiking? It has very tiny hooks that grab hold of anything that happens to touch it. Eventually it falls off in a new location.

This next seed is a milkweed. It is very light with a top that resembles a parachute that allows it to simply float through the air like this (drop a seed).

Isn't it amazing the different ways God has designed seeds so that they can travel distances and start growing some place else?

God not only has made a variety of seeds but he also has made people with tremendous variety. Each one of us looks different, has different interests, different abilities, and different opportunities. You and I should never wish we were like somebody else for each of us is a unique person made by God.

God has special plans for you. He had to create you just the way you are to do that job. Don't try to be like someone else.

And don't look down on others just because they aren't like you. God has made them special and different so that they can be the unique person he wants them to be.

Just as each of these seeds was created differently so they could use a different method to get to a new place to grow, so you and I are each created as unique and different persons. Ask God to help you be the best YOU you can be!

Key Text

"We have different gifts, according to the grace given us." (Rom. 12:6a)

36

God's Plumb Line

Objects Needed

Plumb line (borrow one from a carpenter or handyman in your church).

Theme

God has a standard of what's right and we should be committed to live by that standard.

Presentation

This is a tool you don't see every day. It's called a plumb line or plumb bob. It has two parts to it, a weight and a string. The plumb line has been used as a tool for thousands of years. In fact, it's referred to in the Old Testament.

Here is how it works. When a wall is being built it is important that it be straight up and down. It shouldn't weave in or out. To check the wall, the worker unreels the plumb line and dangles the weight at the end of the string. Of course the string with the weight on it will hang straight down because of gravity. The builders can then see if their wall is straight or not.

God mentions the plumb line in the Old Testament book written by the prophet Amos. He says that he will measure the people to see if they are righteous or not.

God is completely perfect. I'm sure none of us measures up to being perfect. Thankfully God is willing to forgive us when we ask him.

Yet if we want to be called God's children and want to have a close relationship with him, we should remind ourselves that God expects us to act godly. Oh, we may think we are better than so and so and just as good as Joe Blow, but God isn't comparing us to them. God is comparing us to what is right and proper.

When you listen to your parents, Sunday school teachers, and the preacher, and when you read your Bible and listen to your conscience, you are becoming aware of God's standards for you. It's as if he's putting his plumb line up against you.

Remember that God forgives you when you fail him. Ask him to help you be the person he wants you to be. He can help you measure up.

Key Text

"And the LORD asked me, 'What do you see, Amos?' 'A plumb line,' I replied. Then the Lord said, 'Look, I am setting a plumb line among my people Israel.' " (Amos 7:8)

37

The Bible and You

Objects Needed

An old Bible with a small flat pocket mirror glued with rubber cement on a page in the middle.

Theme

When we read the Bible we see ourselves in it.

Presentation

You know what this is, don't you? Sure, it's a Bible. When I open this Bible to read it (have it open just to you), what do you suppose I see? I see myself. What do *you* see when you look into this Bible? (Turn it toward children.) You see yourselves too. That's right. Of course the reason you and I are saying this is because I glued a mirror into this Bible.

But there is another more important way we see ourselves in the Bible and it has nothing to do with mirrors. Just like this mirror, the words in the Bible tell us how we are. When we look at these words and read them or hear them read to us we know God wants us to think hard about them because the Bible is really about us.

Some of the words say that we are making God sad by being bad. It talks about hating people, lying, stealing, disobeying, and many other sins. We do these sins sometimes, don't we?

Other words in the Bible tell us we are loved by God so much that he sent his Son to die for us. How wonderful it is that God loves us that much!

Still other verses tell us how we feel sometimes: sad, discouraged, confused, afraid. Then it says how to deal with those feelings.

You see, God's Word, the Bible, was written for you and me. God wrote it with us in mind. We are to read it, think about it, and then do what it says. When we look into a mirror we see how we need to straighten ourselves up by combing our hair and putting on some good clothes. When we look into God's Word, the Bible, we should also see ourselves and what we must do to be more beautiful persons.

Key Text

"Keep me from deceitful ways; be gracious to me through your law. I have chosen the way of truth; I have set my heart on your laws." (Ps. 119:29-30)

38

Pretzels and Prayer

Objects Needed

A bag of pretzels.

Theme

We should always remember to pray.

Presentation

This is the story of how the pretzel came into being. There was a monk who was the pastor of a church in Italy years and years ago. He had a problem. The children in his church were slow at learning their prayers. So he rewarded the fast learners by giving them a *pretiola* which means "little gift." The little gift was a biscuit shaped like a pair of hands clasped in prayer.

Travelers ended up taking the *pretiola* over the Alps. The Germans glazed and salted them and they became a popular part of the German diet. Then in 1861 Julius Sturgis opened the first pretzel bakery in the United States in Lititz, Pennsylvania. Now pretzels are very popular here too, as you probably know.

We shouldn't forget the reason the monk invented them in the first place: to encourage the children of his church to pray!

To pray to God is a wonderful privilege; we should do it

often. Think about it for a moment. You and I can actually talk to God and he hears and listens! That's what prayer is, talking to God. You don't have to wait until you're in church, at the dinner table, or kneeling beside your bed at night. You can talk to God anytime you want and you can talk about whatever is on your mind.

The next time you see or eat a pretzel I hope it reminds you to pray to God. And now you can each have a pretzel.

Key Text

"Pray continually." (1 Thess. 5:17)

39

Do Life God's Way

Objects Needed

Items used to bake a cake: boxed cake mix, egg, sugar, can of chocolate, bottle of cooking oil, and mixing bowl.

Theme

We should live life God's way if we want it to turn out good.

Presentation

Today we are going to mix up a cake. The instructions say to put the cake mix in a bowl. There. (Throw whole box in bowl.) It says to add one egg so here's the egg. (Throw or place egg in bowl.) Now we need to add some chocolate. (Put can of chocolate in bowl.) Here's some sugar. (Place bag of sugar in.) Now let's add the oil. (Put the bottle of oil in the bowl.)

Well, what do you think of our cake-baking project so far? Not very much? Why? Is it the way I was mixing the ingredients?

I agree with you. I was just having a little fun. I had all the right ingredients but I certainly did not put them together right. However, I had my reason. I wanted all of us to realize that we generally have many of the same things in life. Most of you have enough food, a place to live, some clothing, a few friends, a school you go to, parents or other adults to take care of you. The kids you know probably have most of these same things to make life good.

Yet, it's not enough simply to have these right ingredients to make life good. You must use them right, just like baking the cake.

It's sad but true that many young people have many wonderful things from God but they use them all wrong. They have toys but either treat them so rough they break or are so afraid they will break no one can play with them. They have parents but don't treat them with respect. They may have friends but they don't really want to do what's best for them. They may have a nice house and yard but never pick up their toys to keep it neat or help their parents around the house.

It's not so important what you may or may not have. What is important is that you use what you do have in a right way.

Just as we can use all the right ingredients but fail to bake a good cake, so you and I can have many of the good things of life and ruin it if we don't put it together right!

Ask God to help you use in a good way all of the marvelous gifts he has given you. Then you will create a wonderful life that will be pleasing to you and to God.

Key Text

"Teach me, O LORD, to follow your decrees; then I will keep them to the end. Give me understanding, and I will keep your law and obey it with all my heart." (Ps. 119:33–34)

40

We Need Each Other

Objects Needed

Four sticks from two to three feet in length (trimmed tree limbs or croquet handles will do), eight pieces of string, and a bowl of snack food on a small table.

Theme

God has made us so that we must depend on each other.

Presentation

A man had a dream. He dreamed he was at a marvelous banquet where everyone was seated at a table filled with delicious food. There was only one problem; everyone's arms were tied straight with splints. Let's see how that must have looked. I'll need two volunteers.

Now, let's put a stick from your wrist to your shoulder and we'll tie it at the top and bottom so that your arm can't bend. Then we'll do your other arm and the arms of your friend. (An adult assistant can shorten the time used in this portion of the lesson.)

The problem in the man's dream was that no one could eat because they couldn't bend their elbows to get the food into their mouths. Go ahead and help your-selves to a snack. Do you see the problem they faced?

In the man's dream, one of the people finally found a way they could all eat. Can you figure out what it was? The man who had the idea took a piece of food in his hand and fed it to the person sitting across the table from him. That man, in turn, fed him. Why don't you try it and see if it works. See, it does work!

There's an important lesson here. God wants us to help each other. You need to help others and they need to help you. A person who thinks he or she doesn't really need other people is not very smart. That's not the way God made us.

It's not a sign of weakness to ask others to help you; it's a sign of strength. It takes a big person to ask for and accept help.

Yes, God wants you to help others and to ask others for help. Work together; that's God's plan.

Key Text

"Serve one another in love." (Gal. 5:13)

41

Upside Down Christians

Objects Needed

Cup, pitcher of water, large bowl.

Theme

God cannot fill us with his presence and his good things when we are turned away from him.

Presentation

Would anybody here care for a drink of water? Fine, just let me fill this cup first and then you'll be able to have a cold drink of water. (Have the cup upside down and over the bowl when you pour the water.)

There seems to be a problem. I'm pouring lots of water but the cup is not filling up. What seems to be wrong? (Let a child answer.) Yes, the problem is that I have the cup upside down. Even if I put it under Niagara Falls with all those millions of gallons of water I still would not be able to fill the cup.

Let me turn the cup over and try it again. (Fill the cup.) Now, that's better. The cup simply had to be turned toward the water and it was easily filled.

You know, our God is big and wonderful, ready to give us all kinds of blessings; but we often feel empty, alone, and sad simply because we are turned away from him. We become more interested in so many other things than God, things such as toys, television, playing with friends, school. These things are OK, but we allow them to become more important to us than God. We end up living each day and forgetting about him. What we have really done is turned away from him. It's no wonder we don't feel much of his love and power and wisdom in us. We are like the cup turned away from the pouring water.

The way to turn right side up to God is to think of him often, pray to him, read the Bible every day, and try to act the way he wants us to. When we turn toward God like this we will begin to feel closer to him and to be filled with his goodness just as this right-side up cup is now filled with water.

Key Text

"Blessed are those who hunger and thirst for righteousness, for they will be filled." (Matt. 5:6)

42

Growing Christians

Objects Needed

A child's wall-mounted growth chart or a yardstick.

Theme

We should always be growing as Christians.

Presentation

You may recognize what I have with me today. It's called a growth chart. (Or if it's a yardstick: I want to tell you about a very interesting use for this yardstick.) Parents use it to measure how much their children are growing. Do any of you have a growth chart at home? It's fun to put your initials at the place which shows your height. Then when you come back to it in a few months and mark it again you can see how fast you are growing.

All of you are growing. You will soon be taller than you are now. You will need new clothes and bigger shoes. It's exciting to see yourself grow. I hope you all keep growing for a few more years.

Actually, children are not the only ones here today who are to keep growing. All of the adults need to keep growing, too. I don't mean in physical size, for then we would be giants. But we should all keep growing *spiritually*, growing toward the perfect image of Jesus Christ.

This kind of growth—becoming more Christ-like—is not just for adults but for you as well. Jesus wants you to love him so much, think of him so often, and be so committed to doing what he wants that you become more and more like him all the time.

Let's never start thinking that we are as Christ-like as we should be. We must never stop growing as Christians until we get to heaven and Jesus makes us perfect.

The ways to keep growing spiritually are:

1. Love Jesus, think about him often, and try to do what he wants you to do. Ask for his help.

2. Read your Bible and pray every day.

3. Come to Sunday school and church.

So be a healthy Christian and keep growing!

Key Text

"But grow in the grace and knowledge of our Lord and Savior Jesus Christ." (2 Peter 3:18)

43

Tools of God

Objects Needed

Tools and utensils (for example, hammer, cheese slicer, saw, egg beater, anything with a handle).

Theme

Just as we use tools and utensils to accomplish tasks, so God wants to use us to accomplish his will and purpose.

Presentation

Let's see if you can name these different objects. The first one is easy. What is it and what is it used for? That's right, it's a hammer and is used to pound nails. How about this next item? Yes, it's a cheese cutter and that's exactly what it does. Next, this object? Right, it's a saw used to cut through wood. How about this object? Yes, it's an egg beater, used to beat ingredients while cooking and baking.

Although these tools and utensils are very different in the way they look and in the jobs they do, they have one part in common. They all have a handle. The hammer, cheese slicer, saw, and egg beater all have a handle with which they're held when performing their jobs.

There is one more tool or utensil that I want you to

think about today. It's right here with the hammer, cheese slicer, saw, and egg beater. This other tool or utensil is you and you and you and me!

That's right! You and I can be tools and utensils of God's. There are many good things God wants to do here on earth and he needs your help and mine to do them. He wants to be partners with us. He wants us to be his tools and utensils.

There is one big difference between these tools and utensils and you and me. These objects have no say as to whether they will be used or not. They don't have a mind or a will. We just grab them and use them. But you and I can choose, we can decide if we are going to let God use us or not.

God wants his love, joy, and help to get to your family and friends. He wants to show these things to them through you. Will you act as a person of love, joy, and helpfulness toward the people you know?

Let God get a handle on you. Let him use you as his tool and utensil of goodness.

Key Text

"Offer yourselves to God...offer the parts of your body to him as instruments of righteousness." (Rom. 6:13)

44

The Polished Life

Objects Needed

Two stones: one that has rough and jagged edges and one that is smooth and rounded (a beach pebble).

If you have the opportunity, you may want to collect enough smooth stones from an ocean or lake shore to give each child his own smooth stone. A craft or hobby store may also have a supply of machine-polished stones that could be purchased at a nominal cost.

Theme

Reacting positively to the tough experiences in life polishes us, making us better people.

Presentation

These two stones are quite different from each other, aren't they? This stone has sharp, jagged edges while this one is smooth and rounded. Do you know why there is such a difference between the two?

The rough stone has had a smooth and easy life. It has simply lain around soaking up the sunshine and generally taking life quite easy. Nothing has really bothered it.

The smooth stone, on the other hand, has had a rough time of it. It comes from the water's edge where it has been pushed back and forth, tumbled and ground against other stones. Sand has swirled against it, propelled by the force of mighty waves and currents. All of this pushing, shoving, and grinding has rubbed off its rough edges and made it smooth.

Do you ever feel like this rock? Do you feel like you are pushed around and bumped up against difficulties? All of us do. We all have problems and frustrations.

What we need to remember is that these aggravating experiences can be good for us. I know it's hard to believe that having a friend who lies to you or getting a bad grade or losing a game can be good for you, but it can.

If you ask Jesus to be with you always and to make you strong, you will learn lessons from your troubles and become a better person. If someone has lied to you, you can learn how to forgive that person. A bad grade in school can teach you to study harder next time or not to be so proud of the good grades you usually get that you rub it in to the kids who didn't do so well. Losing a game can show you it's only a game and that losers are also good people.

Bad experiences in life can help us become better people, to become more like Jesus. The next time you have a problem, think about this smooth stone and how, with God's help, your trouble can "polish" you into a better, more Christ-like person.

Key Text

"We also rejoice in our sufferings, because we know that suffering produces perseverance; perseverance, character; and character, hope." (Rom. 5:3–4)

45

The Lift of Love

Objects Needed

A large pail or sturdy laundry basket.

Theme

All of us need the help of others and the Lord to make our lives what Christ wants them to be.

Presentation

I need a volunteer to stand in this pail for a few moments. (Pick a smaller child for the sake of your back, as you'll see.) Now I'd like you to try and lift yourself up. Grab hold of the pail with both hands and lift. (Let the child try.)

There is a very important reason why (child's name) is not able to lift himself/herself up in the pail; what is it? That's right, he's/she's inside it! There's an old saying your grandparents may be familiar with: "You can't pull yourself up by your own bootstraps."

Someone else, someone outside the pail, will have to do the lifting—like this. (Lift the pail, being certain the child takes hold of you for stability.) It's impossible to carry yourself but someone else can do it!

This is not just true for people in pails. It's true for all of us in living our lives. God has made us in such a way that we must depend on the help of others and they must depend on us. None of us has all the strength we need all the time. No one knows everything.

We need other people and they need us. We need teachers, parents, pastors, friends, neighbors, doctors, bakers, fellow church people, and many others. It does not mean you are weak when you need help and ask for it. It means you are smart. You've figured out that God wants it that way.

God's plan is that everybody helps everybody. Don't be afraid to ask for help. And don't be afraid to help someone!

Key Text

"Carry each other's burdens, and in this way you will fulfill the law of Christ." (Gal. 6:2)

46

Gossip Grows

Objects Needed

A decorated "magic gossip box" about $2' \times 2' \times 2'$ in size with a hole large enough for your hand at each end. Locate several objects of which you can find both a small and large size (such as a small screwdriver and a matching large one). Place the large matching items at one end inside the box.

Theme

The negative things we say about people have a tendency to grow way out of proportion as they are shared again and again.

Presentation

Today I want to show you my magic gossip box. Actually, it isn't really magic but we'll pretend it is. Let me show you how it works. I'll take this small screwdriver and put it in this end of the box. Now I'll pull it out of the other end and presto! It's grown into a large screwdriver.

Here's a small flower pot. I'll put it in this end and now I'll reach in the other end and look what we have—a large flower pot!

Here's a small spoon. I put it in this end and when I pull it out of the other end it's turned into a big spoon!

I think you understand why I call this my *magic* box, but let me tell you why I call it my magic *gossip* box: I named it a gossip box because the objects I put into it grow just like gossip does.

Do you know what gossip is? It's when someone tells something bad about one person to another person. It may be true or not, but it usually makes the person talked about look bad.

The even bigger problem with gossip is that when the person who just heard it tells someone else, he might add a little to the story or get it a little mixed up. Then the gossip has grown a little bit bigger. This can happen again and again until the gossip has grown very big.

Gossip is bad. Jesus certainly does not want us to say unkind or cruel things about one person to another. Besides being hurtful it has that tendency to grow each time it's retold.

That's why I call this my gossip machine. It does the same thing to objects that gossip does: it makes them grow bigger.

Let's be more the person Jesus wants us to be and say only kind things about people.

Key Text

"You shall not give false testimony against your neighbor." (Exod. 20:16)

47

Store Up God's Word

Objects Needed

A floppy disk for a computer.

Theme

We should study and remember God's Word so that
we can use it later on.

Presentation

Who knows what this is? That's right! It's a floppy
disk that is used in a computer system. Floppy disks
like this one are used to store information that a
computer has put together. It's recorded on the disk so
that when the computer is turned off or goes on to
other programs, you can take this disk and put the
information back into the computer at a later time. The
information is stored in little sections on the disk called
bytes. Each disk can hold thousands of bytes. You can
look at a disk and you won't see the information
because it's recorded on the magnetic surface. It's
invisible but it's there.

The floppy disk is really a memory for the computer.
It uses the information from these disks to go on and
compute new things.

As great as the computer is and as amazing as a

floppy disk seems, there is something far more amazing—and that's the human brain. It's like a giant computer and it has its own great big floppy disk for storing details called the memory.

There is something that every Christian should store in the floppy disk of his mind so that he can call it up and use it to help him live a better life. Each of us should be storing God's Word, the Bible, in our minds.

If we get into a situation where we are tempted to do wrong we can remember what God's Word has to say about that. Jesus did this when he was tempted in the wilderness. He quoted the Old Testament to the devil. We can also think of something inspiring and helpful in the Bible when we are discouraged or disappointed. But—we won't be able to use the Bible to help us live better lives unless we store it in our minds like a computer stores information on a floppy disk.

How do we store the Bible in our minds? We do it by reading it regularly, going to Sunday school and church where it is preached and taught, and by memorizing Bible verses. Then when we need it God's Word will be right there in our minds to help us deal with that situation to please Jesus.

So, take that marvelous computer we call the mind and store information from the Bible on that floppy disk we call the memory. It will help you be a more successful Christian.

Key Text

"I have hidden your word in my heart that I might not sin against you." (Ps. 119:11)

48

Good Can Come from Bad

Objects Needed

A starfish or a drawing of one on cardboard (and cut out).

Theme

When bad things happen to us the Lord can use it for something good.

Presentation

Do you know what kind of fish this is? That's right! It's a starfish. A starfish is an unusual and amazing kind of fish. Today I want to tell you about just one of its amazing qualities.

If a starfish loses one of its five arms it will grow a new one to replace it.

Years ago in the New England area of our country oyster fishermen hated the starfish because they would eat the oysters. So whenever they caught some starfish in their oyster nets they would cut them up into two or three pieces and throw them back into the ocean thinking they had killed them.

But instead of finding fewer and fewer starfish each year, they kept catching more and more of them! Finally they realized that when they cut a starfish into two pieces both pieces lived and grew new legs so that there now were two starfish. If they cut the starfish into three pieces it formed three starfish. Instead of hurting the starfish population they were helping it.

Isn't it an amazing ability God has built into the starfish so that it can survive and multiply! Though the fishermen thought they were doing something terrible to the starfish, it actually ended up being for the starfish's good.

This same God who made the starfish made you and me. He loves us far more than any starfish. He wants us to have some good come out of the bad things that happen to us.

What are some bad things that happen to us? Perhaps you get a bad grade in school. God can help you use this bad thing for good. He can help you want to try harder next time so you get a better grade. Maybe no one seems to be your friend one particular day. God can help you grow closer to him because he is a friend who will never leave you. Perhaps you get sick and feel terrible. God can help you to remember to be thankful for your good health when you feel well again. Sometimes you get mad at a friend or brother or sister for doing something bad to you. Finally, you have to forgive them if you are going to play together again. By forgiving that person you are becoming a more loving, Christ-like person.

Yes, when bad things happen to us we can turn them around, with God's help, and have some good come as a result, just like what happens to the starfish.

Key Text

"And we know that in all things God works for the good of those who love him, who have been called according to his purpose." (Rom. 8:28)

105

49

The Glove of the Spirit

Objects Needed

A glove and a pen.

Theme

We can't do much on our own, but when the Holy Spirit is within us we can do great things for God.

Presentation

Look at this glove. It doesn't seem to do anything. It just lays here. You can pick it up and shake it and still nothing happens. It can't grasp this pen out of my pocket, let alone write anything. This glove is simply a limp mass of material. It has the shape of a hand but seems unable to do anything a hand can do.

But now watch this glove come to life! When I put the glove on my hand it suddenly has tremendous ability. With my hand inside, the glove can make a fist, walk on two fingers, and even grasp my pen. If we had some paper here it would even be able to write.

Did you know that to God we are like a glove? That's right. And God's Holy Spirit is like the hand that fits into the glove. If we don't invite God to be in our life we are like a limp, useless, empty glove. But if we invite God to come and live inside of us he can begin to do wonderful things. When God's Holy Spirit is within us we have a far greater ability to love others and to understand what is right and wrong and to do that which is right. We also have more peace and joy. We can do all the things we know we should do when God is living inside of us.

The next time you put on a pair of gloves or mittens, think about how your hands can make them do all kinds of things. Then think about the Holy Spirit of God and how he can help you do all kinds of wonderful and amazing things when you let him live inside of you.

Key Text

"But you will receive power when the Holy Spirit comes on you." (Acts 1:8a)

50

God Purifies Us

Objects Needed

Two glasses, household bleach, food coloring, water, and a spoon.

Place a very small amount of bleach in the bottom of one of the glasses so that it is not noticeable. In the other glass mix a couple of drops of food coloring and water. Practice pouring the colored water into the other glass and stirring it. Find the right mixture of bleach and colored water so that the water is bleached clear. The less food coloring you use the more easily it will work. Be sure to keep the liquids out of the reach of children before and after the service.

Theme

God purifies us from our sin.

Presentation

When God decided to create human beings he made them perfect, without sin, just like himself. But people are no longer the way God meant for them to be. Each and every one of us has sinned. That means we have done things that go against what God wants. We have disobeyed him. We are no longer clean and pure.

You could say we are a lot like this glass of water. It is no longer clean and pure either.

But God has done something about the fact that we have sinned and are no longer clean and pure! He sent his own Son Jesus to live on earth and to die on the cross for us. All we have to do now is ask Jesus to come into our hearts and forgive us.

Let's use this colored water to show that God makes us clean. I'm going to take this water and pour it into the other glass and stir it up a little. Look what's happening! The water is becoming crystal clear again!

This is what God does to us. When you ask him to forgive your sins he will do it. You will be clean and pure in his eyes again.

Key Text

"If we confess our sins, he is faithful and just and will forgive us our sins and purify us from all unrighteousness." (1 John 1:9a)

51

Have Faith in God

Objects Needed

A board approximately three feet long and two feet wide. A kitchen table extender will also do.

You will want to choose two strong men from your congregation beforehand to help you. Instruct each man to hold an end of the board so it is level at about six inches from the floor (they should be on their knees). During the lesson choose a small child to stand on the board blindfolded, holding onto your shoulders as you stand nearby. You should start out in a nearly standing position so that the child's arms have to reach up to your shoulders. You can then make the board seem to rise by slowly lowering yourself to your knees so the child's arms reach straight across to your shoulders. Actually he will still be only six inches from the floor. Telling him to jump results in an act of faith and trust in you. You probably will have to really encourage the child to do it, even to the point of holding on to his arms.

Theme

God wants us to have faith in him and when we do he will not disappoint us.

Presentation

Today we want to think about what it means to have faith and trust in God. To do an experiment involving faith and trust I need some help from two men in the congregation. Will they please come forward? Now I need the help of one of you. (Choose a small child.)

First we must blindfold you. Now climb up on the board these gentlemen are holding. For security you may hold on to my shoulders. Just keep holding on. (Slowly lower yourself to your knees; as the child's hands on your shoulders move downward it will give him the sensation of being raised higher, even though the board remains at the six-inch level at the time.)

Now, I want you to trust me and step to the floor. You don't want to do it? Will you do it if I tell you that you're only a small step above it? You have to have faith and trust in me when I tell you it will be all right. Here, let me hold on to you and help you step down. That wasn't bad at all was it? Take off the blindfold and you'll see just how close to the ground you were all the time.

Do the rest of you see what we were doing? Your friend *felt* like he was way up high on the board. I asked him to trust me, to have faith in me, and step down even though it seemed scary to him.

God wants us to have faith and trust in him. Sometimes that's hard to do because we can't see how things will turn out for the good. But God can see. And he will never lie to you. Just as I asked our friend to have faith and trust in me, so God asks us to have faith in him. He can be trusted. He wants the very best for you. He tells us in the Bible what we need to know. We can put our faith in him, because his way always turns out best.

Key Text

"Fear of man will prove to be a snare, but whoever trusts in the LORD is kept safe." (Prov. 29:25)

52

Playing Life God's Way

Objects Needed

A familiar board game with instructions, two pieces of cardboard cut in the traditional shape of the two tablets of stone, and a heart cut out of cardboard.

Write a brief version of the Ten Commandments on the tablet-shaped cardboard. On one side of the heart write "Love God" and on the other side write "Love others."

Theme

Just as it is important to play a game by the rules if everyone is to enjoy it, so it is important for us to live by God's rules if we want to enjoy life.

Presentation

Playing games with your family or friends can be a lot of fun. Here's a board game that I have played. What do you think the writing on the bottom of the box is for (or, on this piece of paper inside the box)? That's right, it's the rules for playing the game.

Can you imagine what it would be like if we tried to play this game without knowing or obeying the rules? It would be terrible, wouldn't it? Everybody would be doing whatever he or she wanted to do. How many of you have ever played with someone who didn't want

112

to play by the rules? It wasn't any fun, was it? In fact, you can't even really play unless everybody plays by the rules. Rules are good to have; they help everybody enjoy the game.

The one who invented life also gave a set of rules to go along with living it. You know who I'm talking about—it was God. Way back in the Old Testament he gave people a set of ten rules that would help them live happier lives. Does anyone know the name of these ten rules? Correct, the Ten Commandments. Here is a list of them. Some of them are: "Honor your parents. Don't murder. Don't steal. Don't lie. Don't wish you had something of somebody else's."

In the New Testament Jesus said the same thing in two basic rules for living. I've written them on this heart because they should *come* from the heart. On one side it says, "Love God the most of all," and on the other side, "Love others as yourself."

Many people don't live by God's wonderful rules and they become frustrated and sad. Always remember and obey the Ten Commandments and Jesus' two rules of loving God and loving others and you will have a happy and good life!

Key Text

" 'Love the Lord your God with all your heart and with all your soul and with all your mind and with all your strength.' The second is this: 'Love your neighbor as yourself.' There is no commandment greater than these." (Mark 12:30–31)

Lightning Source UK Ltd.
Milton Keynes UK
UKOW04f0146020916

281966UK00001B/11/P